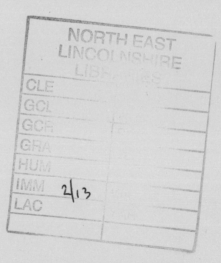

LIVING IN THE WILD: SEA MAMMALS

ORCAS

Claire Throp

Edited by Adam Miller, Andrew Farrow, and Laura Knowles
Designed by Steve Mead
Picture research by Mica Brančić
Original illustrations © Capstone Global Library Ltd 2013
Illustrations by HL Studios
Originated by Capstone Global Library Ltd
Printed and bound in China by CTPS

ISBN 978 1 406 25010 7 (hardback)
16 15 14 13 12
10 9 8 7 6 5 4 3 2 1

British Library Cataloguing in Publication Data
Throp, Claire.
 Orcas. -- (Living in the wild. Sea Mammals)
599.5'36-dc23
A full catalogue record for this book is available from the British Library.

Acknowledgements
We would like to thank the following for permission to reproduce photographs: Alamy pp. 4 (© Danita Delimont Creative), 17 (© nrmarinelife), 25 (© Brandon Cole Marine Photography), 7 (© Streeter Photography); Corbis p. 22 (Minden Pictures/© Tui De Roy); FLPA pp. 13 (Minden Pictures/Norbert Wu), 26 (Minden Pictures/© Flip Nicklin), 36 (Minden Pictures/© Flip Nicklin); Getty Images pp. 11 (Discovery Channel Images/Jeff Foott), 15 (All Canada Photos/Rolf Hicker), 23 (Oxford Scientific/Gerard Soury), 29 (Photographer's Choice/Johnny Johnson), 45 (Dorling Kindersley); Nature Picture Library pp. 10 (© Todd Pusser), 16 (© Wild Wonders of Europe/Aukan), 21 (© Mark Carwardine), 27 (© Brandon Cole), 30 (© Brandon Cole), 33 (© Solvin Zankl), 34 (© Kathryn Jeffs), 39 (© Brandon Cole), 40 (© Todd Pusser); New Zealand Herald p. 38 (APN Images); Photoshot pp. 31 (Norbert Wu), 35 (Francois Gohie), 43 (Juniors Tierbildarchiv); Shutterstock pp. 6 (© lantapix), 19 (© Manamana), 32 (© Minden Pictures), 41 (© Minden Pictures).

Cover photograph of an adult orca with an open mouth reproduced with permission of Superstock/© Gerard Lacz.

Every effort has been made to contact copyright holders of any material reproduced in this book. Any omissions will be rectified in subsequent printings if notice is given to the publisher.

Disclaimer
All the internet addresses (URLs) given in this book were valid at the time of going to press. However, due to the dynamic nature of the internet, some addresses may have changed, or sites may have changed or ceased to exist since publication. While the author and publisher regret any inconvenience this may cause readers, no responsibility for any such changes can be accepted by either the author or the publisher.

Contents

Some words are shown in bold, **like this**. You can find out what they mean by looking in the glossary.

What are sea mammals?

What's that huge, dark shape moving through the water? Suddenly, an orca leaps out of the sea, twists round, and splashes back into the water.

An orca, or killer whale, might look like a large fish but it is a sea **mammal**. Mammals have a backbone, fur or hair on their bodies, and use lungs to breathe. They give birth to live young and mothers feed their babies milk. Does this description sound familiar? It should – humans are also mammals.

Sea mammals live and feed in the sea. There are four groups: whales and dolphins; seals, sea lions, and walruses; manatees and dugongs; and sea otters and polar bears. They are all excellent swimmers and divers. They are also known as **marine** mammals. Marine means "of the sea".

These sea lions watch carefully as orcas swim in the shallow water. Orcas are predators that hunt sea lions.

Meet the sea mammals

There are around 130 different types, or **species**, of sea mammal. They have adapted in different ways to live in the sea:

Type of sea mammal	How do they move?	Where do they live?
Whales and dolphins	use tail, fins, and flippers	These sea mammals live in water all the time.
Manatees and dugongs	use tail and flippers	
Seals, sea lions, and walruses	use flippers	These sea mammals spend some of their time in water, and some on land.
Sea otters	use legs and tail	
Polar bears	use legs	

Cetaceans

Whales and dolphins are **cetaceans**. There are about 90 species of cetaceans, divided into two groups: toothed cetaceans, such as the orca, and baleen cetaceans, such as the blue whale. Cetaceans have very little hair on their body but do have a thick layer of **blubber** to keep them warm. They come to the surface to breathe through a blowhole. Toothed cetaceans have one blowhole and baleen cetaceans have two. Toothed cetaceans use **echolocation** to find prey but baleens do not. Instead of teeth, baleen cetaceans have plates in their top jaw, through which they sieve small prey such as **plankton**.

SIZE DIFFERENCE

Orcas may look huge but they are not very big in comparison to the largest sea mammal, the blue whale. The largest blue whale ever measured was 33.5 metres (110 feet). The biggest ever orca measured only 9.8 metres (32 feet).

What are orcas?

Orcas are the largest members of the dolphin family. Males can grow to lengths of 9 metres (30 feet) and weigh up to 9 tonnes. Females are smaller but can still measure up to 8 metres (26 feet) and weigh up to 8 tonnes. They can reach swimming speeds of up to 55 kilometres per hour (34 miles per hour). However, they usually swim at 5 to 6 kilometres per hour (3 to 4 miles per hour).

Features of orcas

Orcas have large black and white torpedo-shaped bodies that help them to swim fast. They have a strong tail, pectoral fins to help them steer, and a dorsal fin that helps them to balance. A thick layer of blubber helps them to float and stay warm. Their jaws are powerful and they usually swallow prey whole.

Here you can see the size of an orca compared to a human.

Orcas are **social** animals and mainly travel in groups, called **pods**, of up to 40 orcas. They are very good at working together particularly when hunting.

DR MICHAEL BIGG

Dr Michael Bigg (born 1939) discovered a new way of researching orcas in 1972, using photo identification. He realized that orcas can be recognized in photos by their dorsal fin or saddle patch, which are different for every orca. Scientists can now count rather than guess the number of orcas in a particular area and study the lives of individual orcas.

Females and young orcas have small, curved dorsal fins. Males have much taller, triangular-shaped dorsal fins, which can reach 1.8 metres (nearly 6 feet) in height.

How are orcas classified?

Classification is the way that scientists group living things together according to the characteristics that they share. This allows us to identify living things and help us understand why they live where they do and behave the way they do.

Classification groups

In classification, animals are split into various groups. The standard groups are Kingdom, Phylum, Class, Order, Family, Genus, and Species. Animals are given an internationally recognized two-part Latin name. This helps to avoid confusion if animals are known by different common names in different countries. The orca's Latin name is *Orcinus orca*, for example.

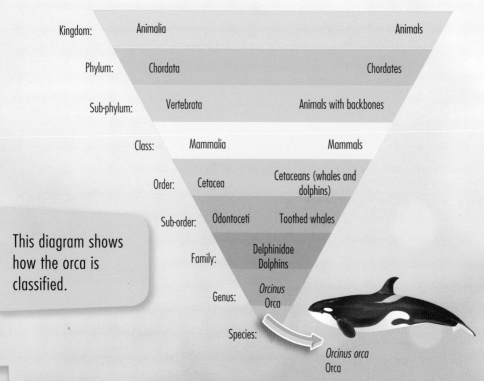

Kingdom:	Animalia	Animals
Phylum:	Chordata	Chordates
Sub-phylum:	Vertebrata	Animals with backbones
Class:	Mammalia	Mammals
Order:	Cetacea	Cetaceans (whales and dolphins)
Sub-order:	Odontoceti	Toothed whales
Family:	Delphinidae	Dolphins
Genus:	*Orcinus*	Orca
Species:	*Orcinus orca*	Orca

This diagram shows how the orca is classified.

Early orcas

At first, mammals only lived on land but around 55 million years ago some moved to the sea – no one knows why. The earliest known orca-like creature was *O. citonensis*, which lived about 2.6 to 5.3 million years ago. It was smaller than the modern orca and was more like a dolphin. Orcas are now classified as *Odontoceti* or toothed whales, of which there are 71 species.

WHEN IS AN ORCA LIKE A HIPPOPOTAMUS?

Until recently scientists thought that cetaceans were descended from hoofed mammals such as cows and horses. Now they think it is more likely that cetaceans such as the orca are distantly related to hippopotamuses! They both have fatty areas in their heads that can give off sounds. They can hear through their lower jaws and there is a close blood match.

This family tree shows some of the whale's distant ancestors.

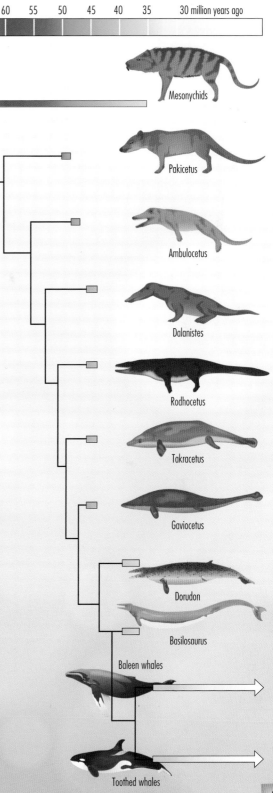

65 60 55 50 45 40 35 30 million years ago

Mesonychids

Pakicetus

Ambulocetus

Dalanistes

Rodhocetus

Takracetus

Gaviocetus

Dorudon

Basilosaurus

Baleen whales

Toothed whales

Types of orca

Orcas living in the Pacific Ocean are well studied and there are three types. **Residents** spend most of their lives in one area. They usually eat fish, such as salmon and herring. **Transients** don't stay in one place for very long. They move around in smaller pods than residents. They travel further for food and eat other sea mammals, such as seals and sea birds. Offshore orcas are the third type, although not as much is known about them because they do not come close to shore very often. They are thought to live in large pods.

Transient orcas, such as these ones, make much less noise than resident orcas.

There is still much to learn about orcas.

How many species?

For a long time scientists have thought that orcas belong to only one species, *Orcinus orca*. But now some scientists are beginning to think that transient and offshore orcas are separate sub-species because they do not seem to mate or mix with the residents. There is a noticeable difference in diet, behaviour, and the shape of their dorsal fin. Orcas in Antarctica have also been divided into three groups depending on their size and diet: Types A, B, and C. Scientists are still not sure whether there are separate species of orca but research continues.

Scientists also believe that orcas are becoming two species in the North Atlantic Ocean around the United Kingdom. Researchers think the orcas can be divided into two groups based on their size, diet, and where they travel. There are a number of obvious differences including the fact that male Type 2 orcas are nearly 2 metres (6 ½ feet) longer than Type 1 males – a big difference!

Where do orcas live?

A **habitat** is the place where an animal lives. The habitat has to provide everything the animal needs from food to shelter. An animal is dependent on its habitat.

Orcas can be found in all the oceans of the world, but usually only in small populations. Orcas have been spotted in tropical waters around Hawaii and Australia, but are more common in colder oceans. Orcas can be seen regularly in the seas around Scotland, Iceland, and Norway. They often swim into areas of thick ice in search of prey in Alaska and Antarctica.

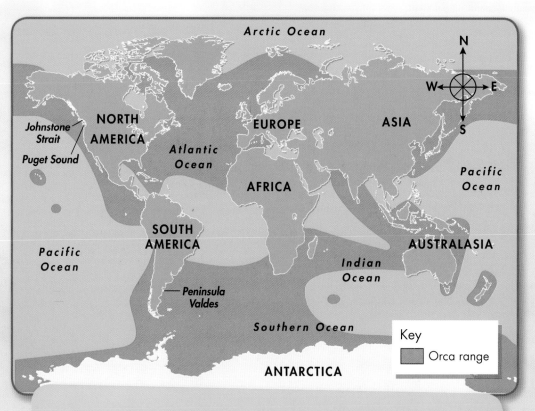

This map shows the main areas where orcas can be found. Some orcas stay in certain areas, such as the southern resident orcas that live in the Puget Sound in the Pacific Ocean.

Offshore orcas have not been well studied but they seem to prefer deep ocean. Most other orcas like coastal waters. They are mainly seen no more than 800 kilometres (500 miles) from the shore where the water is no more than 200 metres (656 feet) deep.

Some oceans are more difficult to live in than others. Orcas living in Antarctica might need to break through ice to breathe.

Migration

Orcas are known to **migrate** long distances in search of their prey. The northeastern Atlantic orcas follow herring, for example. While little is known about offshore orcas, they have been recorded travelling thousands of kilometres in one direction. The movements of orcas can also be affected seasonally by the melting and freezing of pack ice in some oceans.

What adaptations help orcas survive?

An **adaptation** is something that allows an animal to live in a particular place in a particular way. Animals develop adaptations as species evolve over thousands of years.

Body shape

Moving on land is easy because there is little **resistance** from air but moving forward in water is much harder. So orcas have adapted by streamlining their bodies as much as possible. Orcas have torpedo-shaped bodies with a layer of blubber and very little fur or hair.

An orca's tail helps it to move through the sea. The tail has two flat paddles called flukes (see photo). The **horizontal** flukes move up and down to push the orca along. This is different to fish that move their **vertical** tails from side-to-side in order to swim forwards.

The dorsal fin is used partly to help with balance in the water but it has another use: controlling body temperature. When an orca is swimming hard and gets hot, extra heat can escape through the dorsal fin. Some heat also escapes through the tail and pectoral fin.

SKIN GROWTH

An orca's skin grows 290 times faster than that on a human arm!

Blubber

Bodies lose heat around 25 times faster in water than on land. To cope with this, orcas have a layer of blubber on their bodies. The blubber is 7 to 10 centimetres (3 to 4 inches) thick. The blubber is used not only to keep orcas warm but also as a store of food and to help them float in water.

There are no bones in the flukes. This means that some large males have flukes that curve at the edges.

Colouring

The colouring of orcas' bodies helps them to hide. Their bodies are light underneath, so prey looking up from below find it hard to see the orca. They are dark on top so they are less easily seen from above. The pattern also helps to disguise the orca because it breaks up the huge size of the animal. Prey might not feel so threatened because they don't realize its size – until it's too late!

Resident and transient orcas have different diving habits. Transients usually stay under water for longer periods.

Breathing and diving

Orcas have to come to the surface to breathe. The orca has a blowhole (like a person's nostrils) on top of its head so it can take a breath straightaway. When it breathes out, the air is pushed out so quickly that a spray of water shoots into the air. This is called blowing or spouting. The orca closes its blowhole while it is diving under water.

Orcas can dive to depths of at least 100 metres (328 feet). Like other cetaceans, orcas can dive for quite long periods. They can slow their heartbeat from 60 to 30 beats a minute. They save oxygen by pushing it towards the parts of their body that need it most – the heart, lungs, and brain. Orcas can hold their breath for up to 12 minutes but usually their dives do not last more than a few minutes.

Jaws and teeth

Orcas don't chew their food. Their mouths have been adapted for ripping and tearing prey instead. They have large jaws with strong muscles and 40 to 56 teeth. They rip off chunks of prey or swallow it whole.

An orca's teeth measure nearly 8 centimetres (3 inches) long.

Echolocation

It can be difficult to see prey in dark, murky oceans. Orcas have developed a system of echolocation to help them find prey and build up a picture of their surroundings. They make a series of clicks that pass through a fatty part of their forehead called the melon. This focuses the sound into two beams in front of them. The sound bounces off nearby objects and back to the orca. The orca feels the bounces, or echoes, through its lower jaw, which also has a fatty area that joins up with the orca's ear. The echoes tell the orca about the size, shape, and travelling speed of an object as well as other information about its surroundings. **Sonar**, a communication method used by the navy, can confuse sea mammals because it sounds very similar to echolocation.

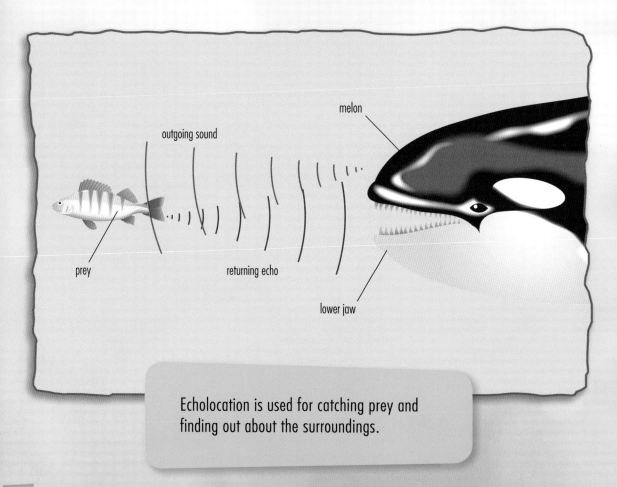

melon

outgoing sound

prey

returning echo

lower jaw

Echolocation is used for catching prey and finding out about the surroundings.

Noise from ships' engines can interfere with orcas' echolocation.

Orcas that eat fish tend to use echolocation more than those that feed on other sea mammals. This is because mammals can hear the clicks made by orcas while most fish cannot. It is possible that sea mammals may have time to escape.

CLICK TRAIN

The series of clicks that orcas make during echolocation are called click trains.

Senses

Orcas have good eyesight both in and out of the water but no sense of smell. As air-breathers that spend most of their time under water, orcas would not be able to use smell effectively. Their hearing is much better than that of humans and they receive many sounds through their lower jaw.

What do orcas eat?

Living things in any habitat depend on each other. This is called **interdependence**. Animals eat other animals or plants in order to get energy. They in turn may be eaten by bigger animals. These links between animals and plants are called **food chains**. Many connected food chains add up to make a **food web**. The more connections there are in a food web, the less it will be affected if one organism dies out.

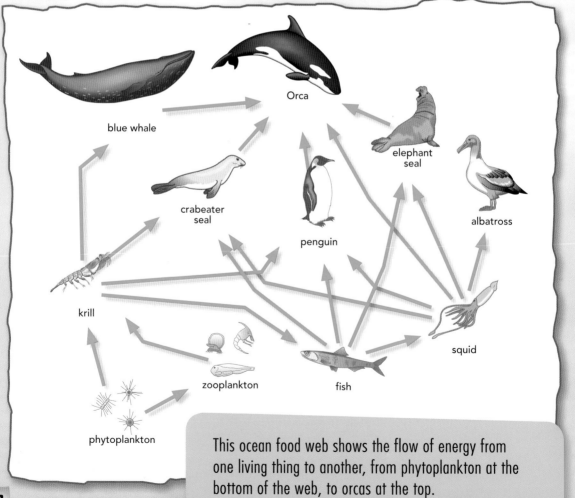

blue whale

Orca

elephant seal

crabeater seal

penguin

albatross

krill

zooplankton

fish

squid

phytoplankton

This ocean food web shows the flow of energy from one living thing to another, from phytoplankton at the bottom of the web, to orcas at the top.

A food chain starts with a plant because plants are the only organisms that can make their own food. They are called producers. In an ocean food web, the producers are plant-like organisms, called phytoplankton, and plants, such as sea grasses. Animals are consumers because they consume, or eat, other animals. Orcas are called carnivores because they eat meat. Animals that eat other animals are known as predators. The animals they eat are known as prey. The orca is the top predator in the sea.

An orca that has successfully caught a herring finds that it attracts a lot of attention!

Finding food

Orcas hunt for food in the water and sometimes on ice or the shore. They have different ways of catching prey, many of which involve teamwork. A pod can chase a minke whale or Dall's porpoise for hours by hunting as a team. One orca chases the prey and then another takes over until the prey is exhausted and can be eaten. Sometimes, however, orcas just follow fishermen and suck the fish off the line leaving only the mouths of the fish behind!

Different diets

Different types of orcas have different diets. Residents eat fish and squid while transients eat sea mammals, such as seals and other whales. The diet of offshore orcas is not known for certain but it is thought that they sometimes feast on sharks. In the northeast Pacific, researchers have seen orcas catch and eat 16 Pacific sleeper sharks in just two feeding sessions.

Playing with food

It is not just human children that play with their food – orcas do, too! Orcas in Argentina come right up to the shore to catch baby sea lions. However, the orca may not eat the sea lion straightaway. The orca flicks the animal up in the air with its tail a few times for fun before finally swallowing it whole.

The diet of some orcas includes fish called stingrays, which they hold on to by the tail.

Sea lion pups are easier to catch than adults.

Sharing food

In the waters around New Zealand, adult male orcas sometimes share their catches with their calves. They catch manta rays, a type of fish, and flip them onto their backs. This causes the fish to relax and not try to escape. The male then passes the ray to his calf or another orca, which then kills the fish. The two share the meal. Orcas living near Norway eat herring. They stun the fish with tail slaps before feeding. They and other orcas then eat the stunned herring.

HOW MUCH DO ORCAS EAT?

Orcas eat 3 to 4 per cent of their body weight in food a day. While it is still growing, a calf needs to eat 10 per cent of its body weight in a day.

What is an orca's life cycle?

The life cycle of an animal covers its birth to its death and all the different stages in between. Sea mammals go through three main stages: birth, youth, and adulthood. Adulthood is when they reproduce and have young themselves.

MEASURING AGE

Scientists have discovered that it is possible to measure the age of orcas by counting growth rings in their teeth, much as we do with growth rings in trees.

Mating

Not much is known about the mating habits of wild orcas. Scientists have mainly studied **captive** orcas. Orcas can mate at any time of year, although some orca populations give birth at particular times of the year. Orcas in the northeast Pacific Ocean, for example, often give birth from October to March.

Orcas do not choose a partner for life. They can have many partners over their lifetimes. In the northeast Pacific, many resident pods join together into a superpod and then socializing and mating takes place.

Orca calves suckle for only 5 to 10 seconds at a time to start with but they do this several times an hour.

Pregnancy and birth

Pregnancy lasts 15 to 18 months before the mother gives birth to one calf in the water, usually tail first. This is so it doesn't drown. The mother pushes the baby up to the surface quickly so that it can take a breath. When a calf is born it is already 2.6 metres (8 ½ feet) long and weighs about 180 kilograms (395 pounds). When it is first born, an orca's dorsal fin and tail flukes are soft and bendy. They gradually stiffen as the orca gets older.

Orca calves **suckle** for at least a year. Their mother's milk has a lot of fat in it to help the calves quickly build up the layer of blubber on their bodies.

Young orcas

Mothers stay close to their calves to protect them. Calves swim in their mother's slipstream, a current of water made as the mother swims. The calf uses less energy when it swims in the slipstream, and this helps it to keep up with the rest of the pod.

Calves remain dependent on their mothers for up to 10 years but most are **weaned** between one and two years of age. Mothers teach their calves how and where to hunt.

Young orcas have plenty of energy for leaping out of the water!

Male orcas help to protect the pod, but have no involvement in looking after their own calves.

The cycle begins again...

Females can become pregnant when they reach the age of 6 to 10 years. Males have to wait till they are big enough to be able to compete with other males. This is usually when they reach about 6 metres (20 feet), around the age of 13. Female orcas give birth every three to five years for around 25 years. When they can no longer have young, the females help out younger mothers with babysitting and teaching young orcas how to hunt.

Orcas have a long lifespan in the wild, particularly females. One female was known to have lived to the age of 90! Most females live for about 50 years and males live for about 30 years.

How do orcas behave?

Behaviour can differ from one pod to another but certain activities are common among almost all orcas.

Pod structure

Unusually for mammals, many pods of orcas stay together for life. The pod is made up of close relatives and is usually led by the mother. Female orcas can have very long lives so sometimes four generations live together. In the Pacific Northwest, male and female resident orcas remain in the same pods they were born into but transient orcas do sometimes leave and can travel on their own.

Positions in a pod can be worked out by aggressive behaviour. Raking or tooth-scratching, when an orca runs its teeth over another orca's body, is common. Head-butting and tail-slapping can also be used.

Social clubs

Orcas form pods of 10 to 20 members but sometimes they join together to form superpods of up to 100 orcas. Researchers think that this is to make and maintain social relationships. The superpods are like social clubs where the orcas can meet other orcas and bond or find a mate. A lot of physical contact, rubbing of flippers, play, and swimming together takes place.

KILLERS OF HUMANS?

Orcas are also known as "killer whales". Up until the mid-1960s they were feared by humans and were often shot. However, there have been no records of a human being killed by an orca in the wild. In fact, orcas have helped humans who have been attacked by sharks. In captivity, there have been cases of orcas attacking their trainers. In 2010, a trainer was drowned when an orca pulled her under the water.

This orca pod is swimming in the Icy Strait in Alaska.

Communication

Researchers use underwater microphones to record the sounds made by resident orcas in the Pacific Northwest. By listening to the pulsed calls, they have discovered that different pods have different dialects. A dialect is a way of communicating that is carried out by a particular group in a particular area. Some orca pods use some of the same calls. These pods are known as clans. Orcas are one of very few mammals apart from humans that use dialects.

Orcas make different types of sounds for different reasons:

Type of call	Reason
Clicks	Used in echolocation to learn about surroundings and find prey.
Pulsed calls	Used to keep pods together and coordinate with other orcas.
Whistles	Used during social activities.

Orcas sometimes slap their tails on the ocean surface and this is known as fluke slapping or lob-tailing.

Common orca activities

Spyhopping, breaching, and fluke and pectoral slaps are all common orca behaviours. Spyhopping is when orcas raise their heads above water to see what's going on around them – particularly useful when hunting. Orcas breach by rising all the way out of the water, twisting around, and returning with a splash. Orcas slap their flukes or pectoral fins on the water to show aggression but sometimes also in play.

SKIN TREATMENTS

Scientists think Antarctic orcas may travel about 8,000 kilometres (5,000 miles) to the warm water of the tropics to get rid of a layer of algae on their skin. The algae build up while the orcas are in the cold Antarctic water and make the orca's skin yellow. Warmer water helps the orcas to shed their skin quickly. When the orcas return from the tropics the yellow colour can no longer be seen on their skin.

A DAY IN THE LIFE OF AN ORCA

An orca's day is made up of hunting, feeding, playing, and snoozing.

FEEDING TIME

Up to 60 per cent of a resident orca's day is spent looking for and eating food. Transient orcas can spend even longer hunting – up to 90 per cent of their day! The way orcas hunt for food depends on where they live. Working as a team, orcas can herd fish, catch seals and sea lions, or even attack large whales or sharks. Some orcas hunt on their own by sliding onto **ice floes** to eat penguins.

Young orcas spend time at a rubbing beach in Johnstone Strait, Canada.

FREE TIME

Many orcas play by tail or fin slapping or breaching, with younger orcas trying for the most adventurous spins and twists. Others have different ways to spend their time. Northern resident orcas visit rubbing beaches. They skim their bodies over pebbles at the bottom of the sea. They may do this to rub off old skin or maybe just for fun!

TIME FOR A SNOOZE

Humans do not have to think about breathing, but orcas have to choose to breathe because they would drown if they breathed under water. When it comes to sleeping, scientists think that an orca may rest one half of its brain at a time so that the other half can control its breathing. This usually happens for just a few minutes at a time but researchers have seen an orca sleep for eight hours before waking. Orcas can rest day or night and usually stay close to the surface while doing so.

When an orca comes up for air, its breath shows up as a fine mist.

How intelligent are orcas?

Intelligence is difficult to measure in animals. It usually refers to how animals hunt and maintain social relationships.

Hunting

Pods hunt through teamwork. Wave washing is one clever way of hunting prey. A pod of orcas dives under the ice. Then they use their tails to make a wave. This knocks a seal resting on ice into the water. Occasionally, the seal manages to escape but three times out of four, the orcas end up with a meal.

Orcas are sometimes called "wolves of the sea" because they hunt in packs like wolves hunt on land. The whale on the right is spyhopping (see page 31).

An orca can stun prey with its tail, which makes it easier to kill.

Orcas on the Peninsula Valdes in Argentina beach themselves to catch sea lions. They have worked out when Southern sea lions go there to have babies. Baby sea lions learning to swim are easier prey than adults!

Orcas sometimes hunt silently so the prey doesn't hear them coming. If they were to communicate as usual the prey would hear their clicks and calls. Instead it is thought that orcas practise their hunting routines before setting off for real. This means that each orca knows where the others will be.

Social skills

The fact that orcas are able to maintain peaceful family and social relationships also shows how intelligent they are. Play is a way for younger orcas to learn how to survive and for older animals it strengthens bonds.

Orcas in captivity have shown that they can learn to do many activities for the watching public. However, many people believe that orcas are too intelligent to be kept in captivity. They get bored and unhappy.

What threats do orcas face?

Pollution is a major problem for orcas because they are the top predators in the sea. Toxic chemicals from farms and industry are washed into the sea and get passed along the food chain. The largest amounts of chemicals end up in orca's blubber where they are difficult to break down. This can cause serious health problems. Orcas may not grow properly, be able to have healthy young, or be able to fight disease. Oil from oil spills can cause eye or skin irritation and is dangerous if swallowed.

Orcas can be damaged by whale-watching boats, so there are guidelines on how close boats should get to orcas.

Noise pollution

Orcas rely on their hearing more than any other sense. Noise pollution from boats, the marine industry, and the military is therefore a major problem. Loud noises can drown out the orcas' calls, making it hard for them to stay with their pod.

Stranding is when orcas are found on beaches. Researchers don't know for certain why this happens but it may be because an orca becomes ill or has an injury and can no longer keep up with the rest of the pod. However, stranding has also been caused by sonar used by the Navy. This disturbs the orcas' echolocation so they become confused and end up stranding themselves. Sonar can also make it difficult for orcas to find prey using echolocation.

IMPROVING AWARENESS

The Whale and Dolphin Conservation Society works hard to make industry and governments aware of the effects of noise pollution on orcas and other sea mammals. In 2012, it criticized a well-known research institute for carrying out underwater experiments with an airgun near Antarctica because of the harmful effect the high noise levels would have on whales and dolphins.

Fishing

Orcas are sometimes injured or killed after getting caught in fishing gear. Purse-seining is a type of fishing that uses a huge circular net to catch fish like mackerel. Many other types of fish – and orcas – can get caught in the net, too. Loss of prey because of overfishing by humans is another threat to orcas. Salmon and cod are common in orca diets as well as human ones. Fishermen themselves can also sometimes blame orcas for damage to expensive fishing gear and loss of their catch. There have been reports of orcas being shot as a result.

INGRID VISSER (BORN 1966)

Ingrid Visser is a marine biologist whose research helped the New Zealand government to reclassify the New Zealand orca to the level of "nationally critical", which means it is **endangered**. She has studied orcas since 1992 and has helped with research projects around the world. Visser teaches people about orcas by appearing in television programmes, giving talks, and writing about orcas.

Captivity and whaling

For many years, orcas were captured and taken to parks and dolphinariums to perform for the public. Fewer orcas are captured now, but sometimes rescued animals can be taken into captivity to provide another animal from which to **breed**. **Conservationists** try to prevent any more orcas being taken into captivity because captive orcas live less natural lives.

Orcas used to be hunted on a small scale for their meat and blubber but less so nowadays. A small number of orcas are still legally hunted for their meat by some Arctic tribes.

Captive orcas do not live as long as wild orcas. They only live into their 20s rather than 30s (males) or 50s (females).

How can people help orcas?

The more scientists learn about orcas, the more they will be able to protect these animals. Unfortunately, it is very difficult to study orcas because they live in oceans. Orcas can be tagged to learn more about where they go, but there is a danger that an orca may be injured when a dart gun is used to attach the transmitter. Also transmitters may not last very long. Orcas can be tracked by the calls they make, but researchers have to get close enough to use underwater microphones.

Learn all you can about orcas and the difficulties they face in the wild. Perhaps you could donate some pocket money or even sponsor an orca.

Conservation organizations

Conservation organizations not only research orcas but also try to make people more aware of the threats that sea mammals face in the wild. Simple things, such as not leaving litter at the beach, can help to protect orca habitats. Oil spills can cause problems for orcas and their habitats. There are ongoing efforts to speed up the clean and rescue times after a spill.

FREE MORGAN

In June 2010, a very ill orca was found off the coast of the Netherlands. Morgan (as she is now known) was supposed to be returned to the wild once she was well, but this has not happened. She has been sent to an amusement park in Spain to be used for captive breeding and performing for the public. Some conservation groups have campaigned to get Morgan released into the wild. Others have argued that past attempts to return orcas to the wild have failed and that Morgan will have a better life in captivity. What do you think?

Here, researchers in Antarctica watch an orca spyhopping.

What does the future hold for orcas?

Healthy adult orcas have no natural predators apart from humans. There are many conservation groups around the world already working to protect orcas and their habitats. Orcas are protected under UK and European Union law and under US law certain orca groups are also protected. However, more needs to be done. The level of pollution in our oceans must be reduced and people need to follow the rules on whale-watching activities. Learning more about orcas can help to focus conservation efforts.

Endangered mammals

It is difficult to know whether orcas are endangered because they are generally difficult to count. It is not even certain how many species there are. Certain populations of orcas can be considered endangered, however. The southern resident orcas that live in the Pacific Ocean around San Juan Islands and the Puget Sound were placed on the US endangered species list in 2005. There are thought to be under 100 orcas in this population. There is now a protected area for these orcas.

It is important that we don't allow orcas to die out. They deserve their place in the natural world. The more young people get involved in their protection, the better. Every little bit helps.

THE PACIFIC NORTHWEST

Orcas living in the Pacific Northwest are the most studied orcas anywhere. Researchers have been following orcas in the Pacific Ocean for over 30 years. They can recognize the orcas and have named them by giving them a letter and number, such as L12.

It is hoped that in the future there will be more protection for the amazing orca.

Species profile

Species: orca

Latin name: *Orcinus orca*

Length: 4.6 to 8 metres (15 to 26 feet) for females; 5 to 9 metres (16.4 to 29 ½ feet) for males

Weight: 3.8 to 8 tonnes for females; 5.6 to 9 tonnes for males

Habitat: all the world's oceans

Diet: fish, squid, penguins, other sea mammals such as seals, sea lions, or smaller whales

Number of young: Orcas usually give birth to one calf every three to five years. Pregnancy lasts 15 to 18 months.

Life expectancy in the wild [average]: around 50 years for females; around 30 years for males

melon

blowhole

white patch
behind eye

sharp
teeth

strong jaw

dorsal fin

saddle patch

pectoral fin

light underside

flukes

Glossary

adaptation body part or behaviour of an organism that helps it survive in a particular habitat

blubber thick layer of fat on a sea mammal's body

breed mate and produce young

captive kept in parks or dolphinariums rather than being allowed to roam free

cetacean name for whales, dolphins, and porpoises

classification sorting of living things into groups

conservationist someone who helps to protect animals, plants, and habitats

echolocation ability to find objects or prey by bouncing sounds off them

endangered describes a species that is in danger of dying out

food chain sequence in which one creature eats another, which eats another, and so on

food web network of intertwined food chains

habitat natural environment of a living thing

horizontal being on the same flat level, like the horizon

ice floe flat area of floating ice

interdependence way in which all of the living things in a habitat and the habitat itself rely on each other for survival

mammal animal that has a backbone, has fur or hair, gives birth to live young, and feeds its young on milk from the mother

marine living in or of the sea

migrate move from one place to another, often at particular times of year

plankton small plants and animals that live in seawater

pod group of whales

pollution harmful waste that can end up in the sea

resident type of orca that spends most of their lives in the same pod in one area and eat mainly fish

resistance force that pushes back when something tries to move forward

social living in groups or communities, in which relationships are maintained

sonar pulses of sound that are used to find prey or learn about surroundings. Machines used by the navy and other organizations can also send out signals similar to those used by orcas.

species group of similar living things that can mate with each other

suckle take milk from a mother's body

transient type of orca that lives in the Pacific Northwest. They eat sea mammals and travel more than residents to find food.

vertical upright, or going straight up and down

wean encourage a pup to eat food other than its mother's milk

Find out more

Books

Killer Whales (Scary Creatures), John Malam (Book House, 2008)

Ocean Wildlife (Saving Wildlife), Sonya Newland (Franklin Watts, 2011)

Whales and Dolphins, Susanna Davidson (Usborne, 2008)

Websites

kids.nationalgeographic.com/kids/animals/creaturefeature/orca/
Learn more about orcas on National Geographic's website.

www.bbc.co.uk/nature/life/Killer_whale
This website includes videos of orcas in the wild.

Organizations to contact

Whale and Dolphin Conservation Society
www.wdcs.org.uk
WDCS is an international organization that aims to protect whales, dolphins, and porpoises from the threats they face. On their website you can adopt a whale or dolphin, give some money to help the charity's work, or learn more about the animals.

Sea Watch Foundation
www.seawatchfoundation.org.uk
Sea Watch works to protect whales, dolphins, and porpoises around the United Kingdom. Their website has information about where to go to see orcas and other sea mammals, and advice on how to spot different species.

WWF UK
www.wwf.org.uk
WWF works to protect animals and nature and needs your help! Have a look at their website and see what you can do.

Index